HIEROGLYPHS

BY JOYCE MILTON

ILLUSTRATED BY CHARLES MICUCCI

GROSSET & DUNLAP • NEW YORK

ANCIENT EGYPT

Almost six thousand years ago, a great civilization grew up in Egypt. The people of this ancient land were ruled by powerful kings called pharaohs.

The Egyptians believed in life after death. Their pharaohs spent much of their wealth building enormous stone tombs. A few pharaohs built tombs shaped like pyramids. The Egyptians also built temples to honor their many gods. They created statues, too – like the Great Sphinx.

Teams of stone carvers and painters often spent years decorating these monuments. They carved messages in the stone, in a form of writing made up of symbols and pictures.

The civilization of ancient Egypt lasted a very long time – almost four thousand years! But eventually it began to decline. There were no more pharaohs. The old ways were forgotten. By 600 A.D. – that's 1,400 years ago! – there was no one left alive who could read the messages carved in the stone.

NILE
RIVER

HIEROGLYPHS

According to one legend, the mysterious symbols were made by temple priests of ancient Egypt who were master magicians. People called the writings *hieroglyphs* - a word that means sacred writing. They believed hieroglyphs were magic spells used by the priests. Anyone who could learn to read them out loud would become a master magician, too.

ROSETTA STONE

Then, some 200 years ago, an old slab of stone was found with a message carved in three different kinds of writing. The top part of the stone contained hieroglyphs. The middle section was even stranger. It was in a form of writing no one had seen before. This turned out to be a simpler form of Egyptian writing, called demotic.

Luckily, the bottom section of the stone was in a language many scholars knew well – ancient Greek. That part could be translated easily.

The slab became known as the Rosetta Stone because it was found near the town of Rosetta in Egypt. It dated from about

ROSETTA STONE

196 B.C., when members of a Greek royal family with names like Ptolemy and Cleopatra ruled in Egypt as pharaohs.

Scholars guessed that the stone bore the same message, written three different ways. Since they already knew what the Greek writing said, they hoped they could use that message to figure out the hieroglyphs.

Learning to read an unknown language is just like breaking a code. But how do you know where to begin?

One place to start is with people's names. People's names often are pronounced more or less the same way, no matter what language they are written in. The Greek writing on the Rosetta Stone contains the name of a pharaoh called Ptolemy. He is mentioned quite a few times.

On the Rosetta Stone, just one name in hieroglyphs appeared inside a cartouche (an oval shape). The scholars discovered that that name was Ptolemy. But what next? How could the scholars go from guessing one name to deciphering the other hieroglyphs?

The man who finally put the pieces of the puzzle together was a Frenchman named Jean-Francois Champollion. Working with cartouches on other monuments, he showed that the hieroglyphs stood for sounds, just like the letters of our alphabet!

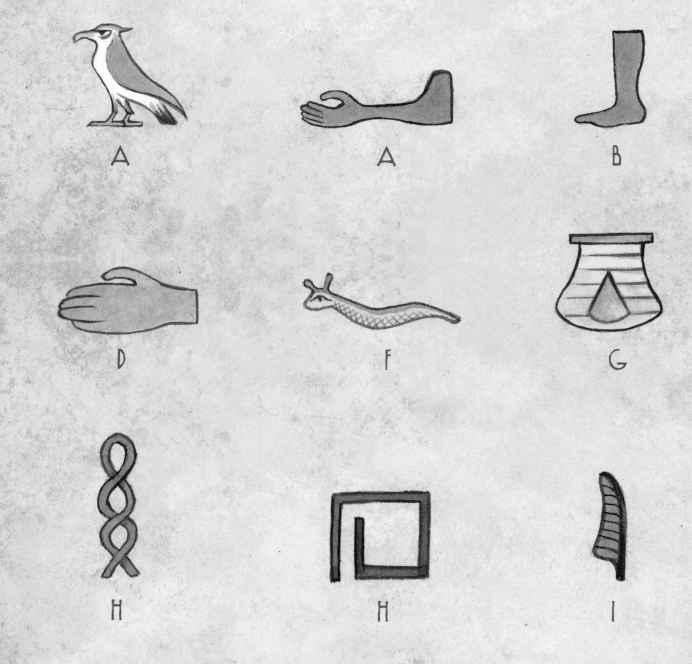

A HIEROGLYPH ALPHABET CHART

This chart shows how to write our alphabet in hieroglyphs. Use it with the stencils at the back of the book to write your name or any message you want.

Twenty-four of the hieroglyphs you see here stood for single sounds. They formed a basic alphabet. The sounds that made up the Egyptian language were not quite the same as the sounds in English. So, the chart shows some shortcuts for making writing with hieroglyphs easier.

One big difference between ancient Egyptian and English is that the Egyptians didn't have an "L" sound. In the chart is an extra hieroglyph – the seated lion – which the Egyptians used when they came upon the letter L in foreign names.

A

A

B

D

F

G

H

H

I

J G

K

L

M

N

P

Q

R

S C

SH

T

TH

W (OU)

Y

Z

WRITING WITH HIEROGLYPHS

Now comes the fun part – using the hieroglyphic alphabet to write messages! Here are some examples of first names:

JOHN=

CODY=

SUSAN=

TIFFANY=

Here's a more difficult name. Can you read it?

On a separate sheet of paper, try out different ways to write your own name.

So far, all the hieroglyphic writing we have seen reads from left to right, the same way we read English. But hieroglyphs can also be written from right to left.

How can you tell in which direction hieroglyphs are written? Look at an animal hieroglyph. If the animal's head is facing left, then the word is meant to be read from left to right. If the head is facing right, start reading on the right.

Ancient Egyptian carvers also arranged hieroglyphs in nice patterns. Below are two different ways to write the name Michael.

MICHAEL=

HIEROGLYPH HINTS

⊙ Spell your name - or any word - the way it sounds. Instead of Michael, think Mykul. Then look for the hieroglyphs that best match those sounds.

⊙ If your name contains repeated letters - like Larry or Ann - you need to print the hieroglyph only once.

⊙ Leave out all "silent e's," like the e in Nicole.

⊙ The vowel sounds in the hieroglyphic alphabet aren't the same as English vowel sounds. Don't worry if you have trouble picking out the vowels for your name. There is no one "right" way.

⊙ Usually, vowels were left out of Egyptian writing altogether. You can leave out vowels, too, especially if your name has a "short e" sound. For Ben, just write:

THE GODS OF THE NILE

Most of the time, the ancient Egyptians used hieroglyphs the way we use letters in writing English – to stand for the sounds that make up words. But not always. Sometimes hieroglyphs were picture clues – one sign stood for an entire thing or idea. For example, each of the many Egyptian gods had its own hieroglyph.

The Egyptian gods were colorful characters. Sometimes they were pictured as animals. Sometimes they took the shape of human beings. Often they looked like a combination of the two. Here are some of the important ones.

OSIRIS

Osiris was a god of the earth and plant life.
He also ruled the Land of the Dead, so he is
usually shown in the form of a mummy.

ISIS

Isis was the wife of Osiris.
She was the protector of children
and a very popular goddess.

SETH, OR SET

Seth, or Set, was the brother of Osiris.
Seth ruled over the desert. In myths,
Seth was sometimes an evil god.

SOBEK

Sobek was the crocodile god.
At Sobek's temple, the priests kept sacred
crocodiles. The crocodiles were treated
well. They even wore jewelry.

ANUBIS

Anubis was pictured as a jackal, or wild dog.
He was the god of cemeteries and of the embalmers
who turned dead bodies into mummies.

BASTET

The Egyptians were the first people to keep
cats as pets. The cat goddess, Bastet, was
associated with joy, happiness, and dancing.

MUMMIES

Egyptian undertakers went to a lot of trouble to preserve the bodies of the dead. These preserved bodies are known as mummies.

One of the first steps in making a mummy was removing the internal organs. Next, the body was preserved with a drying chemical called natron. Once the body was dried out, the undertaker would try to make it look as good as possible. Mummies were buried wearing cosmetics and fancy wigs. The undertaker might put stuffing inside the cheeks to make the mummy's face look more lifelike. Then he placed amulets and lucky charms on the mummy and wrapped it up in yards and yards of white linen.

EYE OF HORUS

The Eye of Horus is a very powerful hieroglyph. The lines under the eye are supposed to look like the markings of a falcon. The falcon was sacred to Horus, a god special to the pharaoh.

The Eye of Horus was a symbol of hope and divine renewal. Eye of Horus amulets often were buried with the dead. Many of them were very beautiful and were decorated with colorful enamels, gold, and jewels. The Eye of Horus also was supposed to protect the owner against the bad wishes of others - against the "evil eye."

The outsides of mummy cases were decorated with hieroglyphs.

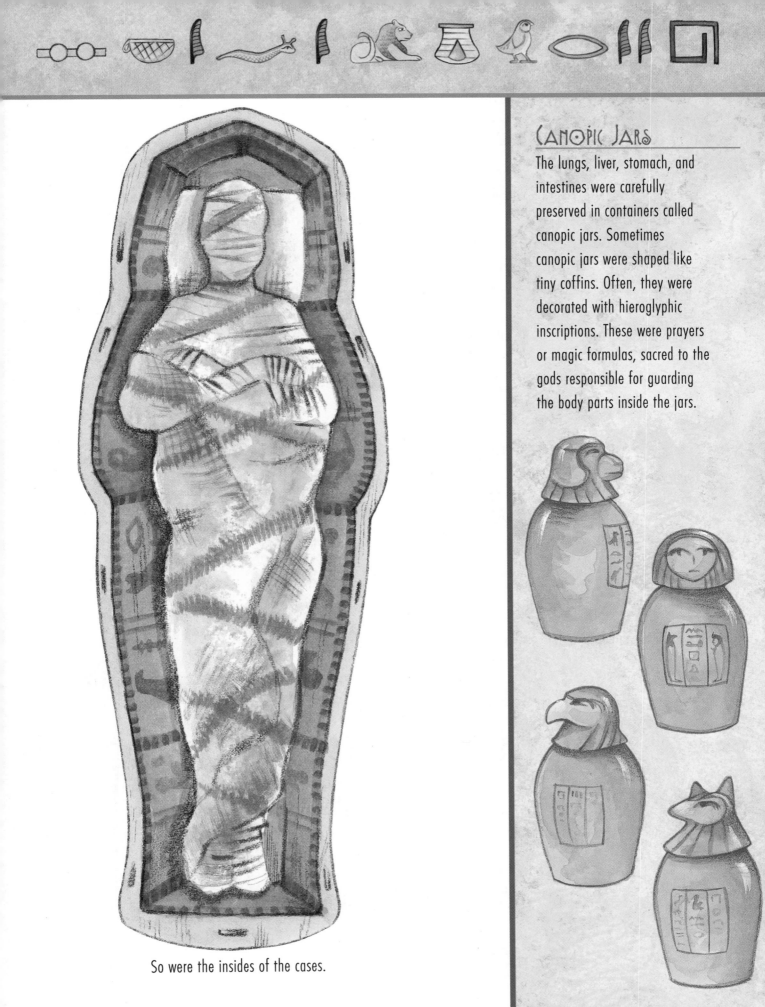

So were the insides of the cases.

CANOPIC JARS

The lungs, liver, stomach, and intestines were carefully preserved in containers called canopic jars. Sometimes canopic jars were shaped like tiny coffins. Often, they were decorated with hieroglyphic inscriptions. These were prayers or magic formulas, sacred to the gods responsible for guarding the body parts inside the jars.

13

DETERMINATIVES

There are about 600 different hieroglyphs in all. You were introduced to some of them in the last few pages.

Now that you know how to write words using the signs of the Egyptian alphabet, you may wonder why the ancient Egyptians needed so many extra signs.

As you know, the Egyptians normally left out all the vowel sounds when they wrote with hieroglyphs. Imagine how words without vowels would look in English. Without vowels, the words man, men, moon, mane, and omen, all would be spelled the same way: mn. How could you tell them apart?

The Egyptians solved this problem by using picture signs. These signs helped the reader determine which word the writer had in mind. For that reason, they are known as determinatives.

If an Egyptian wanted to write the word man, he would add a little picture of a man to the word.

For men, he repeated the picture of the man three times.

Or he just put three little lines under the picture, like this.

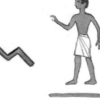

For moon, an Egyptian might add a picture of a crescent moon.

For mane, he might add a picture of a horse.

It was hard to find picture signs for some words. An omen is a sign of something that is going to happen in the future. What kind of picture clue would you use for this word? The ancient Egyptians used a giraffe. Why? Because he is so tall, the giraffe can see things that are coming toward him from far away.

Here are just a few useful determinatives the Egyptians used.

walking, coming

going away

sky

rain

to see

to cry

sun, or a particular day

moon, or month

water, or any liquid

house

used with the name
of a man or boy

used with the name
of a woman or girl

pharaoh

joy

to squash, or to conquer

to carry, or to work

anything to do with hiding

to fall

to eat, drink, or speak

Since you will be using vowel sounds when you write with stencils, you don't need determinatives. Still, it might be fun to learn a few and use them in messages. Most of the ones on these pages are easy to draw.

SCHOOL DAYS

What was it like to go to school in ancient Egypt?

You would not have any books of your own. The teacher might read aloud to you from a primer. Your most important piece of school equipment would be a wooden board covered with a sticky coating called gesso. Hour after hour you would practice writing hieroglyphs, scratching them onto the board with a pointed stick. When there was no more room on the board, you would wash it clean and paint on more gesso. Then you'd be ready to start writing again.

Learning hieroglyphs was hard work. Still, children who got to go to school were lucky. In the Kingdom of the Nile, most people went to work at a very young age.

As far as we know, only boys went to school. Fathers brought gifts to the teachers to make sure there was a place for their sons. Learning to read and write was one way a boy could escape a life of hard labor.

If you were the child of a noble family, you might attend school for a few years in the palace of the pharaoh. Or your parents might hire someone to teach you at home.

TOYS

Egyptian children played with tops and small animals carved out of wood. Some of these animal toys had moving parts - like jaws that could open and shut.

BECOMING A SCRIBE

In ancient Egypt, most people had to depend on scribes to read documents and write letters for them.

Becoming a scribe wasn't easy. To read in English, you need to learn just 26 letters. Egyptian children had to learn about 250 different signs before they could say they knew how to read. Besides the alphabet hieroglyphs and determinatives, there were still more hieroglyphs that stood for combinations of two or three sounds. Scribes had to learn them all.

Once a student had spent a few years scratching his signs on gesso boards, he was ready to move on to writing with a pen and ink. Students usually wrote on pieces of broken pottery. Broken pottery was the scrap paper of ancient Egypt.

Older students eventually moved on to copying down whole sayings as the teacher

read them aloud from a book. Some of the sayings were rules for good behavior. Some reminded the students how lucky they were to be in school.

"The man who makes things out of metal stinks worse than fish roe," one book says. As for the potter, he "grubs in mud more than a pig."

But not all Egyptian writing was so serious. The ancient Egyptians wrote a lot of letters. They also wrote down their favorite stories.

Most scribes finished their education by becoming apprentices. An apprentice wrote letters and kept records. Some scribes traveled with the army. Others went along on trading ships. Becoming a scribe was one way to see the world!

HIERATICS

Just as school children today learn two kinds of writing - printing and script - the children in scribe school learned different forms of writing, too.

Hieroglyphs were beautiful, but they took a lot of time to draw. Most of the time, scribes used a faster, easier kind of writing called *hieratics*.

Hieratic writing changed over the centuries. As time went by, the signs became simpler.

became

became

THE SCRIBE'S LIFE

Most often, we think of the scribe as being a kind of secretary. In Egyptian art, the scribe is shown as a very humble person.

Don't believe it!

The successful scribe was often rich and powerful. He just didn't want to draw attention to how well-off he was. Noble families, the temple priests, even the pharaoh himself, all depended on scribes to keep track of their wealth.

Scribes were in charge of tallying up how much grain was harvested and stored in the noblemen's barns. They collected taxes for the pharaoh and guarded the treasures he was saving up for his tomb.

Some scribes were architects, engineers, and doctors, too. One scribe named Imhotep did all of these things. Imhotep lived about 4,500 years ago. He was in charge of building a great pyramid for a pharaoh named Djoser.

PAPYRUS

When a scribe had something important to record, he would mix up a batch of ink, grab his pen, and write it down on papyrus. The Egyptians did not have paper, but papyrus looked like paper and was very strong. When the scribe made a mistake, he could wipe the ink off the papyrus with a damp rag. Or, he might even use his tongue as an eraser!

MAKING PAPYRUS

⊙ To make sheets of papyrus, the bushy tops of the plants were cut and stripped of their coating. Then they cut the inner part of the stem into long strips.

⊙ The strips were laid out, forming a mat. Then another layer of strips was added, crosswise to the first layer. The layers were pounded with a heavy mallet. Juice oozed out of the papyrus.

Ancient Egyptian books were just sheets of papyrus glued together into long scrolls. These were rolled up and saved in clay jars. If it stayed dry, papyrus lasted a very long time. Some scrolls found in tombs thousands of years old are still in good shape. Parts of these scrolls, even a few whole ones, are in museums today.

⊙ Soon the two layers of strips were mashed together into a single sheet.

⊙ The sheet was pressed under a heavy weight until it was flat and dry.

⊙ Finally, a worker rubbed the papyrus sheet with a flat stone to make it smooth.

23

THE BOOK OF THE DEAD

One of the most popular kinds of papyrus scrolls was a sort of travel guide for dead people.

The ancient Egyptians believed that after a person died, his spirit could live on forever in the Land of the Dead. The Land of the Dead was a happy place where men and women could hunt, dress up, and go to parties, just like when they were alive.

But getting to this happy place wasn't easy. The Land of the Dead was located somewhere in the West, across a great river. Along the way, the dead person's spirit would meet monsters – horrible snakes and lionlike beasts.

To insure a safe journey, some men and women were buried with papyrus scrolls filled with magic spells that could be used to repel monsters. Some of the scrolls also included advice on what to eat and how to travel – even the exact words to say when meeting the many Egyptian gods.

In the Hall of Two Truths, the god Osiris judged the souls of the dead. Thoth, the bird-headed god of scribes, stood nearby, ready to write down the results of the tests.

The dead person's heart would be placed on one side of a balance scale. On the other side of the scale was a feather called maat, or truth. If the heart was free from lies and evil – "lighter than a feather" – the dead person was judged worthy to pass on to the West. But if the dead person's heart failed the test, a monster who was called the Devourer of Shades and who was part hippopotamus and part crocodile, would pounce on him and swallow him up.

WRITING MATERIALS

A scribe kept a little wooden box with cakes of black and red ink and a slot for his pens. Like the paints in a watercolor set, the inks had to be mixed with water before they could be used. The scribe's pen was a stalk from a rush, a kind of grassy plant. He prepared it himself by chewing one end and twisting the fibers into a point.

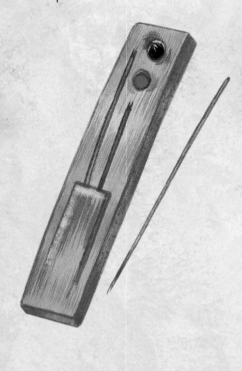

TOMB INSCRIPTIONS AND CARVINGS

Once the spirit reached the Land of the Dead safely, his worries were not over. He still would need all the things he used when he was alive – clothes, furniture, even food. Just like people today save for retirement, the ancient Egyptians saved for the afterlife.

Providing food for the dead was the responsibility of his family. These items were left in a chapel outside the tomb, where the dead person's spirit could find them. But the Egyptians were practical. After a couple of hundred years, there might be no family members left to take care of the dead person's needs. One way to insure that the person wouldn't be forgotten was to have artists paint hieroglyphic inscriptions on the walls of tombs. These were lists of things the dead would need in the afterlife, like bread and beer. The inscriptions called on the gods to use their magic to provide these things.

THE END OF ANCIENT EGYPT

No one in the modern world uses hieroglyphs. In Egypt today, the people have an entirely different system of writing. So why bother to learn these signs at all?

There are lots of reasons. Some people study hieroglyphs just because they like to solve puzzles or because it's fun to have a secret code for sending messages to friends.

But even more important, hieroglyphs can give us a

glimpse of the past. Learning forgotten languages and writing systems is a way of seeing into the minds and hearts of people of long ago.

Hieroglyphs are also beautiful – like so many things Egyptians made. Just look at the objects found in the tomb of the pharaoh Tutankhamen. Cups, chairs, statues – all kinds of beautiful objects were decorated with hieroglyphs.

YOUR HIEROGLYPHS STENCIL

All twenty-four "alphabet" hieroglyphs are on your stencil. Decide what you want to write, and figure out which hieroglyphs you need. Place your stencil on a piece of paper and carefully outline the hieroglyphs you want. You might want to draw a straight line on the paper in pencil to line up the hieroglyphs evenly. You can erase the line after you're done writing. Try to keep the spacing between the hieroglyphs even.

Scribes in ancient Egypt kept a little wooden box with cakes of black and red ink. Nowadays, of course, you can use markers, pens, or colored pencils with your stencil; you could even try using a paintbrush and different colors of paint,  to make it look more ancient. (Be sure to clean your stencil right away before the paint dries and is harder to get off.)

Try writing your name in different cool ways – using different "A" hieroglyphs perhaps, or substituting a "Q" for a "K", as in the "Michael" example on page 9. Write your name from left to right, or flip the stencil over and try writing it from right to left; you can even try writing it from top to bottom! Remember to use the hints on page 9 to make it as genuinely Egyptian as possible.

The pharaohs of Egypt made their names look special by enclosing them in something called a cartouche. These were oval shapes with one flat side, and by encircling a pharaoh's name they showed that he or she was all-powerful. Try outlining the cartouche below and drawing your name in hieroglyphs inside it. Remember, when a word is inside a cartouche, the flat side of the oval should be at the end of the word.

Cartouche for reading left to right

Another thing you can do to make your name look special is add a determinative at the end. Check the list on page 15 for one that might be appropriate, or you can make up your own determinative! If you're a swimmer, you could draw a person in water. Or if you like music, you could draw an instrument or musical notes. Try making determinatives for each of your friends – so that you know which Adam, or which Erica, you're referring to when you write their names.

You can also use hieroglyphs to easily make your own personalized stationery, writing your name on regular 8½" x 11" paper (along the bottom, or in the top corner, wherever you prefer).

If you want to use hieroglyphs to send secret messages to your friends, try rolling your notes into scrolls

the way the Egyptians did, instead of just folding them. You could glue pieces of paper together to make even longer scrolls, and tie them with long grass or ribbons.

Or try making a cartouche out of clay or modeling dough. Then, with your stencil, you can carve your hieroglyphs with a pencil. If you make them out of modeling clay, and then let them dry, these could be great gifts for people. You could also use the clay to make a board the way the schoolchildren in Egypt did; you can practice writing on it, and then "erase" it when it's full and you want to start over.

Most important of all, have fun! Hieroglyphs are beautiful and make any message you write look mysterious and interesting.